DECLUTTERING ADVICE FOR YOUR HOME

Practical Ideas and 101 Tips

Jessica Clarkson

SPECIAL BONUS!
Want this Bonus Book for FREE?

Get **FREE**, unlimited access to it and all of my new books by joining the Fan Base!

SCAN WITH YOUR CAMERA TO JOIN!

TABLE OF CONTENTS

INTRODUCTION

Decluttering your house is a necessary task that can creep up on you. It is not always fun, and it can be a little overwhelming. However, if you leave it for too long it can become an insurmountable problem. "Keep what you use and what makes you happy" is enough guidance for some people. But many of us need a little extra help to decide what to keep and what to get rid of.

The key to decluttering your house is consistently taking baby steps and tackling one area at a time. This way, you can make sure that you are making progress and not just wasting time on unnecessary tasks. There are a lot of different ways to declutter your house. However, what works for one person may not work for another, and what you are willing to do might depend on how much time or money you have.

Hence, the method you choose must be realistic for your situation, so it doesn't feel like too much or too little of an effort. This book will focus on what you can do to get started with the process of decluttering your house or apartment. But let us begin with understanding clutter and how you would benefit from breaking the clutter cycle.

CHAPTER 1

THE 21ST CENTURY CLUTTER SYNDROME

Since we live in a Capitalist world where we are fortunate to easily get everything we need or want by going to a store or simply ordering online, most of us have a problem with too much stuff. Things are more affordable than ever and more easily produced and provided to the consumer. This results in overbuying. Not only is it easy to get whatever our heart desires at any given moment, but there are also deeper reasons why we end up with too much stuff and why it is so hard to get rid of it.

Emotional reasons why we collect "stuff."

It is not just the material items we collect but also who they represent. Our collections give us a sense of belonging and continuity in our lives as it reminds us that there is more to life than what we can see and touch with ease.

- **Collecting stuff to fill a void.**

Sometimes we all feel empty. Some of us have had worse life experiences than others. Maybe you never had the love and attention of a parent. Or you never got to fulfill a dream. And some of us are still dealing with traumas of the past. As humans, we don't like uncomfortable feelings, so our instinct is to quickly replace them. Some people use food or drugs to fill the void but less obvious is the void-filling clutter collectors. What could be easier or more distracting than getting a brand new "anything" that you've always wanted? Think about a more simple life and using positive things to fill any voids in your life. Exercise, healthy eating, a productive hobby are all great ways to feel better without drowning in a pile of clutter.

- **I can't give it away, it was a gift.**

After receiving a gift from someone, many of us are reluctant to declutter. Many people prefer to keep them in storage or on display for fear that their friends will be disappointed knowing how much they don't want it - even if this is true. There is a chance that you may never use a gifted item. Yet people worry about hurting those individuals' feelings by decluttering gifted items, even items that are undesirable for whatever reason (reasons such as there is no room, or you don't need or want it).

- **Letting go of dreams is hard.**

We all have our own dreams or stories to tell, and we don't want those memories or symbols of what has happened in the past, (especially when they are beautiful ones that helped shape who you are today) to go. For example, if someone dreamed about their future as a professional pianist but never acquired enough talent for it, keeping mementos from years ago is vital because it reminds them of where they came from and how far they have come since trying so hard towards this goal. Similarly, it is natural for people to resist throwing away things which symbolize something meaningful in your life (e.g., an old teddy bear). Objects can hold sentimental value beyond just being objects.

- **I spent so much money on this, I can't let it go.**

From price tags to bank accounts, cash is tight for many of us. When money is tight, and one is counting every penny, the idea that we should get rid of expensive objects can seem crazy. But it makes sense. Once an object has been bought with our hard-earned dough, it is very difficult to get rid of it. It doesn't matter how much something costs when it was new. Time changes things, and nowadays, some items may feel like they have lost their value. It may also now be not functional or useful due to changed circumstances or advancements made by society over time.

- **I might need it someday.**

One of the most common emotions for a would-be declutterer is finding objects and thinking, "What if I need this someday?" There are many practical advice tips that you probably have heard before. "If you didn't need it in over a year or two, there is no way you will ever need it." That may be true, but what about mental reasons? Instead of just wanting to keep things because we are afraid they won't exist somewhere else (which can lead us to become hoarders), why not think about how much space these items take up instead?

- **Things are messy; I can never declutter.**

One major emotional issue holding many people back from taking on their clutter headfirst is being overwhelmed when considering how big the job might be ahead. It is enough to deter even those who enjoy cleaning up in general. We often avoid decluttering because we are faced with a large project that seems too daunting. But what you may not realize is, this fear usually comes from an emotional issue like feeling overwhelmed or out of control. So getting rid of your stuff and tackling one room at a time can make it all seem more manageable.

- **The thing has sentimental value.**

When it comes to sentimental items, we have a special kind of dilemma on our hands. How can you choose what is most important when there is only so much space and attention? It is often challenging for people to decide which keepsakes should go up on display in their home or be tucked away where they won't lose sentimentality with age. For example, that little photo of Aunt Hanna from the old days. Do you take out those Christmas cards long ago sent by your friends who now live far-off places like across the country or even internationally? Letting go can be hard, but the freedom you will gain is worth it!

How hanging on to physical things enslaves your mind

You don't have to be a "hoarder" to end up with way too much stuff. Thinking about your stuff all day takes up a lot of energy. Looking at the same pile of clutter every day keeps us stuck. Collecting stuff is a substitute for living your life. Clutter is a pacifier, it keeps us from pushing our comfort zones and healing our voids or traumas of the past. It prevents us from enjoying the simple pleasures of life. This natural state of simplicity and happiness can easily be seen in children before they experience the weight of the world as they grow up.

The extreme situation of hoarding

Before we delve into the extreme hoarding situation, let us understand what hoarding is.

Hoarding is a psychological disorder responsible for making it difficult for individuals to get rid of items, no matter their sentimental value. It can have several adverse effects on the individual and those around them - emotional, physical, social, etc. This can lead one down an unhealthy path with consequences such as financial or legal problems.

What is the psychology behind the process?

People afflicted with hoarding disorder will often collect items that are seen as useless by others. This excessive saving leads to clutter which can disrupt their living and workspaces, leaving them unable to use the space they have available for themselves.

Hoarding vs. Collecting

Hoarding is different from collecting. People who suffer from hoarding disorder collect things like model cars or stamps, organized neatly into collections by type. However, this isn't always what happens when people have hoarded too many objects. When hoarding happens, there is no room for new items and everything just becomes cluttered instead.

It's no wonder why hoarding disorder is a growing problem. Statistics show that it affects men more than women and mature adults over younger ones. It is an unfortunate reality to live with and often leads to major distress among those who have this mental illness.

Hoarding Disorder is thought to be present in 2-6% of the population and has been shown most commonly found amongst older males compared against other demographics like young children or females (which make up less than 5%). Statistics have revealed that people 55 years old or higher are three times as likely to have Hoarders Disorder versus 34-year-olds, making these circumstances quite alarming across all genders.

Signs and symptoms of hoarding

The following are some of the key indicators that can help you identify hoarders.

- People may keep or collect items with little to no monetary value, such as junk mail or grocery bags. One might want to do this because they intend on reusing the item. For example, keeping a paper bag after groceries so it can be reused next time a person goes shopping. Additionally, some people may save things to repair them to fix something themselves rather than paying someone else to do it.
- Unable to let go of their old possessions.
- People can become so stressed about throwing out items that they experience a full-blown panic attack.
- Spend hours trying to decide what items should be thrown out yet fail at it.
- Overprotective about their possessions.
- Live in unusable spaces due to a lot of clutter.
- Stays away from friends and family.
- Unwillingness to give up the possessions.

The downside

Hoarding disorder causes problems in relationships, social activities, and other vital areas of functioning. This may lead to family strain or conflict. And if it gets severe enough, it could also cause health hazards involving tripping or fire risks. More than half of all hoarders have health code violations or fire hazards. Problems such as separation or divorce, eviction, and even loss of child custody may arise from unlivable conditions. Hoarding can lead to serious financial difficulties too.

CHAPTER 2

BREAK THE CLUTTER CYCLE WITH SOME NEW HABITS

Benefits of a clear and clean living space.

The most valuable space is empty space. A decluttered home not only affects your physical well-being but also mental as you feel happier. The benefits of decluttering are endless and will lead you to the most organized space ever.

- **Less stress**

Stress is one of the most common challenges facing people today. Whether it's physical or mental stress, clutter in your home can negatively impact you and make any stressful event even more challenging to manage effectively. One study by UCLA's Center on Everyday Lives and Families (CELF) found that women in messier homes had higher cortisol levels than those living in tidy spaces. Why does this matter? Cortisol affects our health because chronic high levels are linked to various diseases like diabetes, depression, and obesity- so tackling all outstanding tasks could have significant benefits for both your mind and body.

- **More Energy**

Keeping your house clean isn't going to torch as many calories or get you in shape like a HIIT workout. But it implies that there will be moments throughout the week where you are doing some sort of physical activity, unlike sitting on the couch all day long. Experts rounded up a few chores and activities for healthy people:

1) **Washing dishes**: 30 minutes washing plates, bowls, pots & pans (187 cal burned if you are 125 pounds. However, if you are

200 pounds, the calories burned can touch a whopping 300).

2) **Making the bed**: 5 times a week for 30 minutes can burn up to 56 pounds or 25 kg a month.

3) **Washing and folding laundry**: 148 calories per hour.

4) **Vacuuming your home**: 132 minutes each week burs 387 calories.

5) **Scrubbing the bathroom**: 35 minutes of scrubbing the bathroom from floor to ceiling burns as many calories as walking on the treadmill for 35 minutes.

- **More Space**

Decluttering your house can free up a lot of space and make it easier to find what you need. It is beneficial for the environment too because there will be less energy used in manufacturing new goods when old ones are donated. The best way to declutter your house is by getting rid of the things you don't use or need, and believe it or not, this is most of your stuff. This will leave space for more valuable items and help keep your home clutter-free.

- **Boosts Productivity**

Have you ever tried to start a task but found yourself scanning the room for something more interesting? You might be able to blame your space. Disorgani-zation makes it easier and quicker for us humans to find things that require less mental effort. When everything is organized, we can focus on getting stuff done instead of procrastinating. A recent study revealed how our environment directly impacts what catches our attention. So by making sure there is nothing in your work area or home office standing out like a sore thumb, chances are good that you won't pay any extra attention to it at all.

- **Save Money**

After you have decluttered, your home will be a cleaner, simplified environment. You won't have to worry about buying lots of things which make it difficult for you to stay organized. It will be easier to keep a minimalist style in your house without all the clutter. Seeing how little we need can stop us from making unnecessary purchases, and therefore keep our homes neat and tidy. Once you realize how little you actually need, your bank account will be safe from unneeded acquisitions.

- **Get Better Sleep**

Nobody likes to have a nagging, unfinished task lingering on their mind before they go to sleep. When you stop worrying about your dirty dishes or laundry piling up and clean up the house during the day, it leaves you with nothing else weighing down on your brain at night and makes drifting off into dreamland much easier. It is a fact that making sure everything is tidy around bedtime boosts chances of getting quality rest, so don't put off keeping things neat until tomorrow. Do yourself this favor now so all those worries will be out of sight come nighttime. Making an effort every day not only benefits us more than we realize but also does wonders for our mental health as well.

- **Sickness will stay at bay**

A clean home is not only healthy for you but also your family because of the lack of germs, bacteria, dust mites, allergens (and their associated triggers), and other living organisms that can make a person sick. You may not notice it at first glance, but they are lurking in every corner, waiting to attack. A dirty house provides more hiding places for these bugs, leaving less opportunity for them to get attacked by cleaners or sunlight since windows won't open easily when covered with dirt from neglectful cleaning habits. When one thinks about how many hours/days/weeks we spend indoors on average per year and don't forget work, it becomes quite clear just how important this issue is: our homes provide us refuge against all sorts of illnesses.

Top 5 strategies to get started Decluttering

Creating an environment where clutter is less likely to accumulate will help make decluttering easier and more manageable for everyone. But this needs a well-thought-out plan. To help you get over the initial stage of getting started decluttering your house, here are some strategies that may help.

1. Keep, sell, donate, throw away method

Taking an honest look at all the possessions in your home and deciding what is necessary is the key when decluttering. It is vital as it helps prevent clutter from accumulating again since there won't be any new items coming into the house.

Identify and sort.

Categorize everything as you go through each item. This helps you to see what should be kept or tossed without having a mess on your hands later down the line when it is time for storage.

Categories will include clothing, gadgets/electronics (DVDs), books, and games. Go over each category and sort the items into four piles: keep, toss, sell or donate.

- **Keep:** The tips in the next Chapter will help you decide what to keep. Find a special spot for each item that you are keeping and make sure it always gets returned to that spot.

- **Donate:** Make sure all your donated items are in a cardboard box and labeled "donations" so that you can drop them off at the Goodwill or Salvation Army where workers can make use of your unneeded items.

- **Sell:** Craigslist has become the go-to website for listing items online. It is not only easy to list your item, but people on Craigslist are more likely than other sites such as eBay and Amazon to buy what you are selling. The main reason is the close location of the buyer and seller. Sellers can also get a lot of attention from buyers by using creative titles or pictures in their listings.

- **Throw away:** As soon as you fill up one garbage bag, take it out and dispose of it correctly by placing it in the dumpster. Or take to the curb yourself if there is no public service available. This will ensure that you are not going through your trash and reconsidering your choices. Additionally, for old televisions and electronics that are made from hazardous materials like lead - make sure they go straight into recycling facilities. These places are capable of dealing with these harmful substances appropriately before being recycled back into something new.

2. Make storage look good

When you have a cluttered house, it can be hard to keep feeling organized and neat. If your home is looking like an unorganized mess, use some creative strategies to organize items that remain on shelves or counters. For instance, consider using decorative jars for spices instead of storing them all disorganized with other items such as cooking oils. Also, an old chest turned into a coffee table would also work but make sure its contents are hidden from view.

3. Ask for help

Decluttering your whole house can be a daunting task for one person. Luckily, you can ask family members or friends to help with tasks that seem too demanding on their own. Even if it is just picking up and putting away some items, so they are not in the way as you declutter, a helping hand/hands will make everything easier. And having another opinion is often helpful when deciding what should stay or go from an old item we might have been hesitant to get rid of before now. I suggest not asking the people you live with for help since they are likely to want to keep things. If you are having a really hard time getting started you can always hire a professional.

4. Devise a naturally decluttered environment

It won't always be as hard as it is in the beginning. If there is a certain place where your items seem to pile up more often, think of ways to stop that from happening again next time around. For example, suppose junk mail is piling on top of one another and taking over the coffee table or kitchen counter space. In this case, I recommend setting an organized recycling bin by those specific locations so every piece of paper gets tossed before the pile could get any bigger.

5. Form a new habit to declutter regularly

You are not alone if you are feeling overwhelmed by the mess in your home. It happens to even the most diligent of homeowners, but it doesn't need to be a stressful experience. Instead of letting clutter frustrate you, try committing yourself to occasional "mini-decluttering" and cleanups. It can be accomplished once a month or once every year. You can download the free Declutter Printable

Time Log offered at the beginning of this book, to help get you started.

CHAPTER 3

101 TIPS TO SAY GOODBYE TO CLUTTER

1. Work Solo

Although in most cases, rallying your kids or husband to help, when decluttering I suggest doing it on your own. Other family members will inevitably want to hang on to things that are unneeded and quickly forgotten.

2. Have a quarantine area.

If you are getting rid of toys or other family members' items, have a room, cupboard, garage area or attic where you can store these items for 1-6 months to see if they are missed. If someone asks for it, you can return it or gauge the level of attachment and say you're not sure where it is, you will look for it later, or that it has moved on to a better place.

3. Have a game plan.

Set some goals, this week the bedroom, next week the kitchen. Write them down and put them on the wall. Try to follow your plan. Whether you are clearing out your belongings to downsize or simplifying your life, decluttering is a daunting task. But it can be done in stages. Focus on one room at a time rather than everything all at once. Lists are a great way to plan your decluttering journey, you can list each room or each drawer and cross it off when you have finished.

4. Color coding is helpful.

If you are using the four-category technique: Keep, Sell, Donate and Throw Away. Each category can be denoted with its own color. It can be as easy as a black garbage bag for trash, a blue recycling bag for donations and so on.

5. Start with items you definitely don't want to keep.

Look around, it's not too hard to find things that you simply do not use! The spare this or that, an extra coffee maker that was given to you as a gift or a pair of shoes that you have and never will wear. Start with easy give-aways.

6. Spring cleaning can happen anytime!

No need to wait for Spring. Don't use "waiting for Spring" as a reason not to start today! By the time Spring comes around your house will be perfect and you can enjoy the Spring weather doing something else besides cleaning.

7. Have some Fun!

No need to be sad about your decluttering job, put on some music and order your favorite dinner. You can also use your timer, ask a friend to come over and help or do it quickly and get some exercise at the same time!

8. Take pictures of treasured items that don't make the cut.

When getting rid of my kids' baby items, I had difficulty letting go of my child's first car seat. Keeping this giant keepsake is not practical, so a photograph can easily be stored and is the next best thing.

9. Be sure to pace yourself.

Decluttering your home doesn't have to happen all in one day. Set aside one night a week or a weekend morning. Try to set goals that you can achieve in one sitting. If decluttering a drawer is what you can accomplish in one evening, that's great! But starting a job and coming back in a week is a waste of time because much time is just spent orienting yourself and having to start over is not productive.

10. Get some boxes and garbage bags.

Boxes are best for keeping and selling piles, while garbage bags work great for trash and donation items.

11. Your home is not a storage unit.

There is a reason why people pay for storage units, all that space is worth money! Keeping something you may or may not need someday is like paying for space that you could use for something else.

12 . Less is More.

The most valuable space is empty space. Once you have your items down to the essential and most important to you, you will see the peace of mind and serenity created by non-cluttered, empty space.

13. Give yourself permission to buy again.

If you're having trouble letting go of something that is easily found online or at a store, tell yourself, if you need it in the future, you will just go and buy it!

14. Touch it once.

When sorting or organizing, try to put the item where it belongs, keep, throw away, sell, or trash piles. Sort the mail as you get it, junk mail in recycling, bills on your desk. Putting it in a pile just makes extra work for you to do later.

15. Ask yourself if it's "the best or your favorite."

Do you have too many bathroom towels? Or too many mugs in your kitchen? Choose your absolute favorites to keep.

16. Ask yourself if the item is "useful or beautiful".

Having the absolute best of everything in your house will ensure no valuable space is taken up by second-rate stuff.

17. Ask yourself if it sparks joy.

This is one of Marie Kondo's favorite deciding questions to determine what stays and what goes. Eventually, you will create a home environment specific to your likes, it will be your oasis of joy.

18. Don't be afraid to re-gift.

Sometimes we hang on to things because they were given as a gift, if you haven't used them, think about passing them on. Giving it to someone that can use it is a win-win situation.

19. Give every essential item a "home".

Giving every essential item its own spot will help you notice clutter when it creeps in. Keep essential items in their home and get rid of everything else.

20. Keep a box in your closet.

Make it easy for yourself to declutter your wardrobe, each day you are looking at your clothes and find something that you no longer wear, pop it in the box!

21. Use the "Ex Test."

A little trick to see how important things are to you. Ask yourself if you would contact a despised ex (romantic or other) to get the thing back. If you would not, then the thing is not that important.

22. Ask yourself "would I buy it now?"

Sometimes we end up with things we just don't need or use. If you didn't have it, would you go out and buy it today? If your answer is no, then say goodbye.

23. Learn to love the minimalist look.

Once you have one clear space, learn to love the minimalist, decluttered look. Be mindful of clutter when it appears and get rid of it immediately!

24. Use the hanger trick.

Take everything in your closet and flip the hangers the other way. Whenever you wear something, change the hanger back to the regular way. Mark a date on your calendar, 6 months is a good time period for clothes. If the hanger is still backward, it's time to donate.

25. Gifts for others.

Instead of just thinking about what you can get rid of, start thinking about what others can use.

Books, kitchen supplies, clothes, many others would be grateful for and love to use what you no longer need.

26. Tackle paper-stacks.

Give yourself 3 options: shred, file, recycle. Each paper you pick up will have one of these fates. If you think you may need the information but not the paper, take a photo and store it in a digital file and recycle the paper.

27. Try the 10 percent method.

If you have a really hard time getting rid of something you love to collect, mugs for example. Gather them all together and start by donating 10% of your collection.

28. Take everything out of your medicine cabinet, shelf, or drawer.

We all have a space where expired medications live on forever. Take everything out of this area and trash expired medication, organize bandaids and other essentials, and don't be afraid to toss creams, ointments, or bottles that no one uses. Discard any outdated medicines, makeup products, skincare items that are not being used anymore.

29. Pace yourself.

Baby steps, the journey of 1000 miles begins with one step. Don't tire yourself out, start a little at a time, you never know when your decluttering superpower will kick in and you won't be able to stop. Do a little at a time and take small steps by focusing on one zone (like kitchen cabinets) before moving on to another area. This will make things less overwhelming as well as rewarding when finished.

30. Organize your clothes closet by type and color to avoid duplicate items.

You may not realize you have 5 black tank tops or 3 red dresses, put them in order of color in your closet so you can keep your favorites and pass on others. Start by sorting out every piece of clothing into categories, like shoes or dresses. This will make it easier and less overwhelming while completing these daunting tasks.

31. You can't take it with you.

All of us are on this planet for a limited time. What will happen to your stuff when you are no longer here? It will be moved on to someone that can use it. There is no time like the present to pass your stuff on to someone that can use it.

32. Limit your stuff.

Choose one category to work with, for example, bathroom towels, if they are spilling out of the cupboard and stuffed in sideways, it's a good indication that you need to scale back on that category.

33. Purge BEFORE you organize.

Don't even think about buying bins or baskets until you are down to your absolute favorite last-cut stuff. If you don't, you will end up organizing things that you don't need and create a lot of extra work for yourself.

34. You shelved it for a reason.

You might find an item hidden at the back of a shelf that makes you think maybe you can use it now. No. You put it there for a reason, pass it on to someone that will love it.

35. Just because you've had something for a long time doesn't mean you have to keep it.

Use the "beautiful, joyous, favorite" criteria to decide if you are keeping it. Take a photo if you think you might want to remember it in the future.

36. Just because it is valuable doesn't mean you have to keep it.

All the more reason to try to sell it and make some money. Sometimes we keep things because they are valuable, or "might go up in value". Don't use this reason to keep anything. Pass it on to someone who can use it now, and try to make some money at the same time.

37. Get rid of kitchen duplicates.

Do you really need 3 cutting boards or 2 waffle irons? Pick the best one and give the rest to

Goodwill. At the same time, get rid of plastic utensils, extra napkins and ketchup packets. You will never use them.

38. Think about selling some more valuable items.

Don't get too stuck in thinking you have to sell everything. Many things just don't have value these days because of cheap manufacturing. But some items you can post in places like Facebook marketplace, craigslist, Kijiji. Make a rule, like only 10% of your stuff you will try to sell, the rest in a box and gone!

39. Practice one-in-one-out.

You have worked so hard to have less stuff in your house. Use this rule to keep it that way. If you bring in some essential piece of something, be sure to pass on another piece to goodwill or the trash.

40. Use the 90/90 rule.

The Minimalists' have a 90/90 rule. They suggest asking yourself if you've used the item in the last 90 days and if you will use it in the next 90 days coming up. If the answer is no to both, then get rid of it. 90 days is arbitrary, you can use 6 months if you prefer.

41. Use tape to declutter your kitchen.

Use masking tape or washi tape to find out what you actually use in your kitchen. Put a piece of tape on each item, then when you use it, peel off the tape. Mark on your calendar, 3 months or 6 months, then check for everything with tape still on it that hasn't been touched.

42. Clear out extra shower bathtub products.

You don't need 5 kinds of shampoo or conditioner. Trash the ones you don't use and don't buy anymore. Keep only your favorite soaps and skin products. The same goes for sponges, scrubbers and other body care items.

43. Go on a decluttering binge.

Find some empty boxes to place around your house, this might inspire you to start filling them. Once filled, put them in your car or at least on your porch so that you aren't tempted to return anything to your home.

44. Designate a box for incoming papers.

Papers make a big mess, here there and everywhere, choose a box and put every single paper that comes in your house in the box until you have time to properly dispose or file them. You can even put some file folders in your box. A recycling bin or bag nearby will help when it's time to sort.

45. Learn to file quickly.

If you are using files in your paper box, learn to sort papers quickly, garbage, recycling, household bills, other, etc...

46. Start with one area.

Start with one clutter-free area. Make sure nothing gets put in there! Eventually, this clear space will spread to your house. If you declutter a little here and there, you won't notice much difference, but when you can look back at a certain decluttered area, it will inspire you to continue. Just be diligent about keeping your clutter-free areas clutter-free!

47. Think about what you gain by letting go.

By decluttering your living area you gain space, time, and energy, freedom, among other things. Less is more, you will feel weightless and free with less stuff

48. Clear off a counter.

One clear counter is a good place to start practicing your new de-cluttering skills. Once it's clear be mindful to keep it clear. It will get easier the more you practice.

49. Pick a shelf.

Choose one shelf to start with, clear it off completely and put back only essential items. Make a promise to yourself to keep it that way.

50. Schedule a decluttering evening or weekend.

You might need to put your decluttering session on your schedule. If you are a busy person, definitely schedule in an evening or weekend to get some work done. You can involve your family and friends as well. However, I find that when others help they always want to keep things.

51. Choose 5 things, and find places for them.

A place for everything and everything in its place, Choose 5 important things that you are keeping and find a good place for them. Promise yourself that you will keep the spot just for that item.

52. Spend a few minutes visualizing the room.

Take some time to just sit and think about what is essential in the room that you are working on. How would it look with clear surfaces? What can you pass on to the donation box?

53. Create a "maybe" box.

If you are wondering about giving up some items, you can put them in the "maybe" box and put them in your quarantine area. Put some tape with the date on them and put the box in your quarantine area (basement, garage, attic) to see if anybody misses any items. Then when 3 or 6 months is up, you can pass it on for donation. Out of sight out of mind usually works.

54. Use a 30-day list for buying new items.

Half the battle with clutter is not buying new things. When you have the desire to buy something, put it on the list, if you still need it after 30 days, then the item must be important or essential. You will be surprised at how many things are unneeded and you've had them on your 30-day list.

55. If you haven't worn it in 6 months, you probably never will.

Every time you are in your closet, look for something to add to your closet donation box. If you haven't worn it in 6 months chances are you never will. If you haven't worn it in a year, then you definitely never will. Don't hoard your old clothes. Donate them to a donation center or consignment store to help someone who needs it.

56. Dump everything out of a drawer.

Just dump it, place the things back in the drawer that belong there. Everything else is either trash, for donation or belongs somewhere else.

57. Have a conversation with your significant other (SO) or roommate.

If you live with a collector of clutter, you will want to have a talk with them. Explain what you are trying to do and that you will really need their help. Then give them this book to read themselves!

58. Clear surfaces.

The most common place to put stuff is a flat surface, this is also the best place to keep clear for your new uncluttered look. Once you are down to your essential items. You can put everything else in a drawer, hang it on a hook, or put it in a cupboard. Keep those surfaces clear!

59. Pretend you're moving.

A little mind trick, pretend you have a week to pack everything up into moveable boxes or bins. Get to work to lighten your load.

60. Work at your own pace.

Everyone's lives and schedules are so different so you will need to do what works for you. Whether you use a list, schedule time for decluttering, or just do it whenever you can fit it in. Do what works best for you and your household

61. Find hidden storage spaces.

If you have a small living space, you can find places like under your bed or on top of cupboards, to hide things you use seasonally or for special occasions. Under the stairs or behind doors can house racks or different kinds of organizers to keep important items out of sight.

62. Make a place for clutter to go.

Sometimes clutter enters our home and we are just too busy to deal with it. Have a box in your hallway closet for new clutter that needs to be sorted. This way you can get to it when you have time and keep your home clutter-free at the same time.

63. Declutter in stages.

If tackling one room at a time isn't working for you. Do a sweep of your whole house and collect items for the trash or donation box. Once you have less stuff everywhere, you can work on one room or space at a time.

64. Create a clutter-hotspot list.

Some areas are clutter hotspots. The table inside your front door, the counter by the phone, the bathroom counter, your nightstand or coffee table. Make a list of these areas and add it to your regular weekly cleaning routine. These spots need some extra effort.

65. Use baskets.

Get some decorative baskets for each room, through any little items that are essential but can easily be mistaken for clutter in them. Then find an out-of-the-way place to put the basket.

66. Think vertical.

A multi-coat hanger on the back of a door or a bar added in your kitchen for hanging utensils off will keep items off your counter or other surface and create more clear surfaces and more space.

67. Some things just don't belong in the kitchen.

To make your countertops a cleaner, more organized space, you should first move any items not used every day off the counters. This leaves only what is needed on hand and eliminates clutter for an easier to clean area.

68. Pass on items to a good cause.

If you think of the people that can benefit from your extra stuff, it will be easier to give some of it away. Women's shelters, Goodwill, domestic violence shelters, Thrift stores, habitat charities, etc. are all wonderful ideas.

69. Make your bed every day.

Doing this routine daily will help you feel more organized and clutter-free. It's a great way to start the day. You will feel much more accomplished once you have dealt with one of the most daunting tasks in any bedroom-cleaning endeavor.

70. Use hooks to keep hats, scarfs, etc.. from piling up.

Easy to remove no-stick hooks are great and can be put anywhere to keep small items from forming their own pile.

71. Edit your decor.

If you have a lot of decorative items in your home, pillows, vases, etc.. you can put some in the closet and switch it up from time to time. Or give away your least favorite of these items.

72. Use of over-the-door pocket shoe organizers.

Great for storing slippers, toys, shoes and all kinds of other items. You can use them in the bathroom, laundry room, kids rooms or pantry.

73. Use a timer.

If you're having a hard tie getting started decluttering, use a timer. Set it for 5 minutes to start and work your way up to 10 minutes, 30 minutes and eventually an hour of decluttering time. Use your printable Time Log to keep track of your progress.

74. Take before and after photos.

Start by taking a photo of your cluttered area, once you start decluttering it can be hard to see the progress when you are immersed in organizing, have a look back at your before photo to feel like you've accomplished something.

75. Use labels.

Putting labels on items will remind everyone where the items live. For example, a hairbrush could have a bathroom drawer label, to help remind all family members to put things back in their place.

76. Use clear storage bins.

This will save you time because you don't have to rummage through the whole bin to find something. You also don't have to label the bin because you can easily see what is inside.

77. Battle clutter with a 15-minute nightly clean-up.

This is a good habit to get into and will make sure you start the next day in a clutter-free, tidy environment. It will also help you have a restful, worry-free sleep. If night-time isn't a good time for you, choose a time that suits your schedule, just be sure to spend a few minutes each day working towards your clutter-free goal. Use a Time Log to help you keep track.

78. Repair broken items and clothes, or finally get rid of them!

Sometimes we keep broken things with the best of intentions. As you go through your area decluttering, move the broken items into your car so you can drop them off to be repaired. If they don't leave your car within a week drop them off in the garbage bin. This goes for clothes too, if you can't get them to the tailor to be mended, put them in the trash or pass them on to a charity that can repurpose them.

79. Cut back on cleaning supplies.

Many cleaners do the same thing and also a multi-purpose cleaner can take the place of three or four bottles and cleaners. Also, you don't need multiple sponges, brushes, etc, pick the best ones and pass the rest on.

80. Buy clutter-hiding furniture pieces.

A captain's bed with drawers underneath, a bench that opens up, or a coffee table with drawers are great places to hide clutter.

81. Say "no" to multitasking.

When you start decluttering an area, make sure you are free of distractions. Focus on your task at hand and set your timer if you have another issue trying to pull you away.

82. Make a catch-all box or bin near your front door.

One bin can hold your keys, sunglasses, random mail and many other things that come and go until you have a chance to sort through them. The entry is the first thing people see when they walk in, so make sure it's always tidy and welcoming.

83. Don't worry about making a mess before you get organized.

Decluttering is definitely one of those things that gets worse before it gets better. When you dump out a drawer or empty out a cupboard don't worry about throwing everything in a pile. This is step one in getting organized.

84. Get mad at your stuff!

You might need to have a grown-up fit and get really mad at all the junk taking up your space and energy. Get to work to find these things a better place, away from your home.

85. Make the thrift store or Goodwill a part of your weekly routine.

Before you do your weekly grocery shopping or any other weekly activity, add in a stop at the Thrift store or Goodwill. Drop off whatever you have collected throughout the week. This will motivate you to add to your box or bag throughout the week.

86. Create a profile for selling stuff on your local seller's website or Facebook Marketplace.

Be proactive! Even if you don't have anything to sell quite yet, get ready. Just knowing that you're all set up and ready to post something might just motivate you to pass on some items to people that need them and you can make some money at the same time!

87. Declutter kids' artwork.

All those drawings, paintings and endless coloring pages can build up. Keep it all in one place, go through and choose your favorites to feature on the wall. Choose pieces that your child put a lot of work into and has a personal connection with. Eliminate coloring pages and scribbles and save the rest in a bin. Come back in 6 months to give the artwork bin another go through and try to eliminate some pieces that don't seem as important as they once did. You can also photograph some of it to store digitally.

88. Declutter kids' toys.

Keep the toys in order. Assess each toy for wear and tear. Ask yourself: do your kids play with this one anymore? If not, recycle or store the old ones away until you have a garage sale. Some tips for storing the toys your kids are keeping are: get a bed with drawers underneath, use a toy hammock and use stackable clear labeled bins.

89. Don't spend more than 5 minutes on one item.

One simple tip that is really helpful when you are decluttering is to never spend more than five minutes deciding on a single item. If you can't decide what to do with an item, put it in the "maybe" box or your quarantine area to see if you need or miss it.

90. Have a garage sale.

You can team up with a neighbor to help motivate you and bring more people to your sale. Try to do this without kids or your SO in case they disagree with getting rid of toys or other items.

91. Declutter your nightstand.

Your nightstands are a hot zone for clutter, so open up the drawers and start clearing out anything that doesn't belong to them. Books you have read or broken glasses should be thrown away to declutter your space as much as possible before putting things back neatly into their respective places.

92. Group similar items together.

Instead of storing similar items in multiple places, keep them all in one place so you always know where to find them. This will help you to see if you have duplicates so that you can choose your favorites and pass the rest on. For example, by keeping all your shoes and boots together, you can see if you have duplicates and pass them on to others.

93. Don't forget to focus on the big stuff, too.

You may have ended up with too many shelving units or armchairs. How many do you really need? Free up some valuable space by putting them up for sale.

94. Decluttering is a skill that can be learned.

Somehow you got yourself into a cluttered situation. So breaking free of these habits doesn't happen overnight, be patient with yourself. Use the Time Log to log your decluttering time as well as some new habits that replace buying or bringing new items in your home.

95. Clear out your book collection.

You might be surprised when you start looking through your books, you might not remember getting some books and have no intention of ever reading them. Time to put them in the Thrift store or Goodwill box.

96. Have a catch-all basket in the living room

Instead of keeping remote controls, magazines, and books scattered across the coffee table, find one small basket where you can store these items in a more organized fashion.

97. Get rid of mismatched food containers.

Give up hope that you will find the missing counterpart. Also storing them WITH the lids on will make sure you never lose them or get mismatched lids/bottoms again.

98. Get rid of old technology.

This includes fax machines, old gaming systems and old phones. They will never come back in style. If you are throwing out old electronics, be sure to recycle them at the appropriate recycling depots. It's as simple as a quick Google search for locations near you. Find out where the local electronics recycling is in your town and go there often!

99. If you are stuck, hire a professional to get you started.

Have a look on Facebook or Google to find a professional declutterer or organizer. They will be happy to help and the cost is definitely worth it.

100. Just say "no" to more stuff.

If you find yourself buying things to fill a void, try getting some new habits. If you get temporary happiness from your new purchase only to regret it the next day, it's time to replace your buying habit with something more positive. Exercise, a new hobby, reading, healthy eating, puzzles, gamebooks are just a few healthy replacement suggestions.

101. The easiest way to organize your stuff is to get rid of most of it!

Helpful words from The Minimalists. It is impossible to organize your home and your life when you are swimming in never-ending stuff that constantly moves around and needs to be organized. It is like trying to clean up during a tornado. Embrace the minimalist lifestyle, keep only your favorite and best of each necessary item. Have a designated spot for each. Pass the rest on to someone who needs it, it is a win-win situation.

CHAPTER 4

OTHER RESOURCES

You may also consider using information from other resources, such as the few mentioned below.

Netflix

Professional organizer and best-selling author of The Life-Changing Magic, Marie Kondo became an instant sensation with her acclaimed Netflix show, "Tidying Up with Marie Kondo". Her methodology focuses on moving through personal spaces in categories (rather than room to room). Clothing is categorized separately from books or papers. Even if they are found together. This includes everything from furniture to kitchen appliances as well. These five different categories include clothes, books/papers (including magazines), miscellaneous items like toys & small electronics (that belong nowhere else but don't quite fit into another category for sentimental reasons alone). Finally, the most coveted objects: things you love enough to keep forever despite their condition.

Marie Kondo's approach to decluttering is more than just the physical act of tossing things out. Before anything goes, she asks you to physically hold the item and look at it. Ask yourself "does it spark joy?" Discard it if there's no spark but thank your possessions for their service before letting them go.

The Minimalists

One of the Minimalists favorite approaches is to have a "Packing Party". It is based on the thought that why not make your decluttering journey enjoyable? With this decluttering philosophy, you can invite friends over and order pizza while packing up all of your possessions into boxes for moving as a party activity. After three weeks (or longer), most of these items will still be packed away because they don't provide any value to life. You may then donate or sell them - depending on their condition, or simply trash them when finished with the process.

Facebook Marketplace

Facebook Marketplace is a new and exciting way to buy or sell your items. It is so easy, too; you can either post an item for sale, reply to someone who has posted their listing of desired goods, or "swipe" through other people's posts until something catches your eye. The coolest part of this applica-tion is that it doesn't require downloading any extra apps. All transactions are done in the Facebook Messenger App, which most people already have on their phones.

Professional Organizers and Declutters

If you are having a hard time with it all but you know you want to change, don't be afraid to get some help.

CHAPTER 5

LOG BOOK

DECLUTTERING LOG BOOK

How to Use the Log Book

Hello! Welcome to your own Decluttering Log Book. There are a few ways to use this Log Book to help you to simplify your life. Once your house is clutter-free, you will be shocked at how much free time you have. All the time spent organizing endless things in your home is suddenly now free to spend doing enjoyable things.

Here are some Tips on how to use the Log Book to keep yourself focussed on action towards a clearer, cleaner, decluttered home:

1. Print the Yearly Time Log Pages, you can 3-hole-punch them and put them in a Duotang or binder. You can also use a stapler.

2. If you are planning to do weekly decluttering instead of daily decluttering, I suggest you get a highlighter and mark each Friday, for example, according to your yearly calendar.

3. If you prefer to log each day that you declutter and not follow the daily Log, you can print multiple copies of the last page and easily write in the date that you are decluttering.

4. You do not have to wait until January 1st to start, either print the whole Log Book and start where you are in the year, or just print the pages for the dates where you are in the year when you receive this book and get started decluttering.

5. You can print this book year over year and keep going. Clutter is never-ending and you will always have to keep on top of it.

Thank you for downloading this book, and may your year be clutter-free!

DECLUTTER
DAILY TIME LOG

	TIME SPENT	ACHIEVEMENTS
JANUARY 1		
JANUARY 2		
JANUARY 3		
JANUARY 4		
JANUARY 5		
JANUARY 6		
JANUARY 7		
JANUARY 8		
JANUARY 9		
JANUARY 10		
JANUARY 11		
JANUARY 12		
JANUARY 13		
JANUARY 14		
JANUARY 15		
JANUARY 16		
JANUARY 17		
JANUARY 18		
JANUARY 19		
JANUARY 20		

DECLUTTER
DAILY TIME LOG

	TIME SPENT	ACHIEVEMENTS
JANUARY 21		
JANUARY 22		
JANUARY 23		
JANUARY 24		
JANUARY 25		
JANUARY 26		
JANUARY 27		
JANUARY 28		
JANUARY 29		
JANUARY 30		
JANUARY 31		
FEBRUARY 1		
FEBRUARY 2		
FEBRUARY 3		
FEBRUARY 4		
FEBRUARY 5		
FEBRUARY 6		
FEBRUARY 7		
FEBRUARY 8		
FEBRUARY 9		

DECLUTTER
DAILY TIME LOG

	TIME SPENT	ACHIEVEMENTS
FEBRUARY 10		
FEBRUARY 11		
FEBRUARY 12		
FEBRUARY 13		
FEBRUARY 14		
FEBRUARY 15		
FEBRUARY 16		
FEBRUARY 17		
FEBRUARY 18		
FEBRUARY 19		
FEBRUARY 20		
FEBRUARY 21		
FEBRUARY 22		
FEBRUARY 23		
FEBRUARY 24		
FEBRUARY 25		
FEBRUARY 26		
FEBRUARY 27		
FEBRUARY 28		
FEBRUARY 29		

DECLUTTER
DAILY TIME LOG

	TIME SPENT	ACHIEVEMENTS
MARCH 1		
MARCH 2		
MARCH 3		
MARCH 4		
MARCH 5		
MARCH 6		
MARCH 7		
MARCH 8		
MARCH 9		
MARCH 10		
MARCH 11		
MARCH 12		
MARCH 13		
MARCH 14		
MARCH 15		
MARCH 16		
MARCH 17		
MARCH 18		
MARCH 19		
MARCH 20		

DECLUTTER
DAILY TIME LOG

	TIME SPENT	ACHIEVEMENTS
MARCH 21		
MARCH 22		
MARCH 23		
MARCH 24		
MARCH 25		
MARCH 26		
MARCH 27		
MARCH 28		
MARCH 29		
MARCH 30		
MARCH 31		
APRIL 1		
APRIL 2		
APRIL 3		
APRIL 4		
APRIL 5		
APRIL 6		
APRIL 7		
APRIL 8		
APRIL 9		

DECLUTTER
DAILY TIME LOG

	TIME SPENT	ACHIEVEMENTS
APRIL 10		
APRIL 11		
APRIL 12		
APRIL 13		
APRIL 14		
APRIL 15		
APRIL 16		
APRIL 17		
APRIL 18		
APRIL 19		
APRIL 20		
APRIL 21		
APRIL 22		
APRIL 23		
APRIL 24		
APRIL 25		
APRIL 26		
APRIL 27		
APRIL 28		
APRIL 29		

DECLUTTER
DAILY TIME LOG

	TIME SPENT	ACHIEVEMENTS
APRIL 30		
MAY 1		
MAY 2		
MAY 3		
MAY 4		
MAY 5		
MAY 6		
MAY 7		
MAY 8		
MAY 9		
MAY 10		
MAY 11		
MAY 12		
MAY 13		
MAY 14		
MAY 15		
MAY 16		
MAY 17		
MAY 18		
MAY 19		

DECLUTTER
DAILY TIME LOG

	TIME SPENT	ACHIEVEMENTS
MAY 20		
MAY 21		
MAY 22		
MAY 23		
MAY 24		
MAY 25		
MAY 26		
MAY 27		
MAY 28		
MAY 29		
MAY 30		
MAY 31		
JUNE 1		
JUNE 2		
JUNE 3		
JUNE 4		
JUNE 5		
JUNE 6		
JUNE 7		
JUNE 8		

DECLUTTER
DAILY TIME LOG

	TIME SPENT	ACHIEVEMENTS
JUNE 9		
JUNE 10		
JUNE 11		
JUNE 12		
JUNE 13		
JUNE 14		
JUNE 15		
JUNE 16		
JUNE 17		
JUNE 18		
JUNE 19		
JUNE 20		
JUNE 21		
JUNE 22		
JUNE 23		
JUNE 24		
JUNE 25		
JUNE 26		
JUNE 27		
JUNE 28		

DECLUTTER
DAILY TIME LOG

	TIME SPENT	ACHIEVEMENTS
JUNE 29		
JUNE 30		
JULY 1		
JULY 2		
JULY 3		
JULY 4		
JULY 5		
JULY 6		
JULY 7		
JULY 8		
JULY 9		
JULY 10		
JULY 11		
JULY 12		
JULY 13		
JULY 14		
JULY 15		
JULY 16		
JULY 17		
JULY 18		

DECLUTTER
DAILY TIME LOG

	TIME SPENT	ACHIEVEMENTS
JULY 19		
JULY 20		
JULY 21		
JULY 22		
JULY 23		
JULY 24		
JULY 25		
JULY 26		
JULY 27		
JULY 28		
JULY 29		
JULY 30		
JULY 31		
AUGUST 1		
AUGUST 2		
AUGUST 3		
AUGUST 4		
AUGUST 5		
AUGUST 6		
AUGUST 7		

DECLUTTER
DAILY TIME LOG

	TIME SPENT	ACHIEVEMENTS
AUGUST 8		
AUGUST 9		
AUGUST 10		
AUGUST 11		
AUGUST 12		
AUGUST 13		
AUGUST 14		
AUGUST 15		
AUGUST 16		
AUGUST 17		
AUGUST 18		
AUGUST 19		
AUGUST 20		
AUGUST 21		
AUGUST 22		
AUGUST 23		
AUGUST 24		
AUGUST 25		
AUGUST 26		
AUGUST 27		

DECLUTTER
DAILY TIME LOG

	TIME SPENT	ACHIEVEMENTS
AUGUST 28		
AUGUST 29		
AUGUST 30		
AUGUST 31		
SEPTEMBER 1		
SEPTEMBER 2		
SEPTEMBER 3		
SEPTEMBER 4		
SEPTEMBER 5		
SEPTEMBER 6		
SEPTEMBER 7		
SEPTEMBER 8		
SEPTEMBER 9		
SEPTEMBER 10		
SEPTEMBER 11		
SEPTEMBER 12		
SEPTEMBER 13		
SEPTEMBER 14		
SEPTEMBER 15		
SEPTEMBER 16		

DECLUTTER
DAILY TIME LOG

	TIME SPENT	ACHIEVEMENTS
SEPTEMBER 17		
SEPTEMBER 18		
SEPTEMBER 19		
SEPTEMBER 20		
SEPTEMBER 21		
SEPTEMBER 22		
SEPTEMBER 23		
SEPTEMBER 24		
SEPTEMBER 25		
SEPTEMBER 26		
SEPTEMBER 27		
SEPTEMBER 28		
SEPTEMBER 29		
SEPTEMBER 30		
OCTOBER 1		
OCTOBER 2		
OCTOBER 3		
OCTOBER 4		
OCTOBER 5		
OCTOBER 6		

DECLUTTER
DAILY TIME LOG

	TIME SPENT	ACHIEVEMENTS
OCTOBER 7		
OCTOBER 8		
OCTOBER 9		
OCTOBER 10		
OCTOBER 11		
OCTOBER 12		
OCTOBER 13		
OCTOBER 14		
OCTOBER 15		
OCTOBER 16		
OCTOBER 17		
OCTOBER 18		
OCTOBER 19		
OCTOBER 20		
OCTOBER 21		
OCTOBER 22		
OCTOBER 23		
OCTOBER 24		
OCTOBER 25		
OCTOBER 26		

DECLUTTER
DAILY TIME LOG

	TIME SPENT	ACHIEVEMENTS
OCTOBER 27		
OCTOBER 28		
OCTOBER 29		
OCTOBER 30		
OCTOBER 31		
NOVEMBER 1		
NOVEMBER 2		
NOVEMBER 3		
NOVEMBER 4		
NOVEMBER 5		
NOVEMBER 6		
NOVEMBER 7		
NOVEMBER 8		
NOVEMBER 9		
NOVEMBER 10		
NOVEMBER 11		
NOVEMBER 12		
NOVEMBER 13		
NOVEMBER 14		
NOVEMBER 15		

DECLUTTER
DAILY TIME LOG

	TIME SPENT	*ACHIEVEMENTS*
NOVEMBER 16		
NOVEMBER 17		
NOVEMBER 18		
NOVEMBER 19		
NOVEMBER 20		
NOVEMBER 21		
NOVEMBER 22		
NOVEMBER 23		
NOVEMBER 24		
NOVEMBER 25		
NOVEMBER 26		
NOVEMBER 27		
NOVEMBER 28		
NOVEMBER 29		
NOVEMBER 30		
DECEMBER 1		
DECEMBER 2		
DECEMBER 3		
DECEMBER 4		
DECEMBER 5		

DECLUTTER
DAILY TIME LOG

	TIME SPENT	ACHIEVEMENTS
DECEMBER 6		
DECEMBER 7		
DECEMBER 8		
DECEMBER 9		
DECEMBER 10		
DECEMBER 11		
DECEMBER 12		
DECEMBER 13		
DECEMBER 14		
DECEMBER 15		
DECEMBER 16		
DECEMBER 17		
DECEMBER 18		
DECEMBER 19		
DECEMBER 20		
DECEMBER 21		
DECEMBER 22		
DECEMBER 23		
DECEMBER 24		
DECEMBER 25		

DECLUTTER
DAILY TIME LOG

	TIME SPENT	ACHIEVEMENTS
DECEMBER 26		
DECEMBER 27		
DECEMBER 28		
DECEMBER 29		
DECEMBER 30		
DECEMBER 31		

DECLUTTER
DAILY TIME LOG

DATE	TIME SPENT	ACHIEVEMENTS

CONCLUSION

Decluttering is a way of editing your home. Since your home's story is constantly being written, decluttering is always an ongoing task. The reward at the end is that your home will contain only the things that you enjoy and that are useful to you. Remember this final goal to keep you going when you are feeling discouraged. Eventually, you'll be surrounded by things that make you happy and that are in your house just for you! The good news is, once the extra and unnecessary stuff that you don't need is gone, only the best stuff is left.

The result of decluttering is that you have a cleaner, less cluttered, and simplified home. It is more likely to be organized and easier to clean as well. And therefore, your house will remain tidy without the constant upkeep required by an overstuffed space. Plus, it feels great. You can get started on this project right now using the useful tips you have learned! We hope they help make your life just a little bit simpler!

Printed in Great Britain
by Amazon

18571289R00058